Vegan Meal Prep for Beginners 2019-2020

5-Ingredient Affordable, Quick & Healthy Budget Friendly Recipes | Save Your Time, Heal Your Body & Live A Healthy lifestyle | 30-Day Meal Plan

Barbin Koten

By reading this document, the reader agrees that under no circumstances are we responsible for any losses, direct or indirect, which are incurred as a result of the use of information contained within this document, including, but not limited to, errors, omissions, or inaccuracies.

Table of contents

Introduction

Just a decade ago, veganism was generally regarded in a negative light.

Vegans were considered bizarre and plant-based diets were thought to belong to the realm of nonconformists and tree-hugging radicals.

But times have changed.

While it may seem like veganism is just one of the many healthy diets on trend, research indicates that the demand for plant-based options will continue to rise as people become more aware of the profound effects our food choices have on our health, the environment, and sustainability of food sources.

If you're on a vegetarian diet, making the switch to the vegan diet is relatively easy.

Of course, it's also possible to go from being an omnivore to being vegan. You just need to pace yourself so the transition will not be too drastic or difficult.

In this eBook, you will learn the basics of veganism.

You will also learn how meal prep can help you stick to this lifestyle in a sustainable manner.

This way, you don't have to save yourself inside the kitchen for long hours each day preparing meals. You simply have to prepare in one batch, and then reheat whenever it's time for your meal.

Convenient, delicious, easy and healthy—what more can you ask for?

Let's get started!

Chapter 1: Vegan Made Easy

What is Veganism?

According to the Vegan Society, veganism refers to "a way of living that attempts to exclude all forms of animal exploitation and cruelty be it for food, clothing or any other purpose." In other words, the vegan diet is a plant-based diet and eliminates the consumption of eggs, dairy, and any product that comes from animals.

While dietary veganism is restricted to the non-consumption of animal products, other forms of veganism eliminates that use of animal products, such as silk, leather, fur, and wool.

Why Vegan?

People who decide to go vegan do so for several reasons, one of which is to stand against cruelty to animals. This is because modern farming practices often mean animals live in tight cages and pens under generally deplorable living conditions.

In addition, many vegans are against the killing of animals for the purpose of consuming the meat.

Another reason why many people switch to veganism is to protest the environmental impact bought about by raising livestock. Compared to the production of plant-based alternatives, animal agriculture requires the use of more resources and leaves a higher carbon footprint.

Better health is one other major factor why veganism has become more popular in recent years. Vegan diets have been linked to lower body mass index and lower body weight. A plant-based diet has also been associated with lower risk of heart disease, cancer, and cognitive impairment like Alzheimer's.

Benefits of Vegan Diet

Veganism may seem too restrictive for many, but proponents believe the benefits outweigh the challenges of having to find meat-free alternatives to meals that they were used to eating.

Benefit # 1 - Good overall health

A diet that eliminates animal products and animal fats improves overall health in the following ways:

- Non-consumption of animal fats, such as trans fats and saturated fats, which raise the level of LDL or bad cholesterol in the body leads to lower risk of heart disease and certain cancers.
- By avoiding the consumption of animal products, vegans avoid chemicals and environmental toxins that may be transferred to humans through animal fats.
- Because the vegan diet is naturally rich in fiber and focuses on the consumption of whole grains, it can help lower blood sugar levels.
- A plant-based diet that includes probiotics could also reduce arthritis pain as it can lessen inflammation and improve the body's ability to absorb nutrients.

Benefit # 2 - Improved physical fitness

When a balanced diet is followed, vegans are likely to be more physically fit than their meat-eating counterparts.

One of the reasons why is because the vegan diet is often packed with nutrients that support the recovery period of the muscles in between trainings. Because of their consumption of extra nutrients and elimination of saturated fats, vegans typically have better levels of endurance and enjoy more flexibility.

There is also lower tendency for injuries as the diet does not contain foods that weaken the tissues and bones.

Benefit # 3 – Better weight management

Animal products are higher in fats, which equates to higher calories. Because animal sources are eliminated from the diet, vegans are likely to be better at managing their weight. In other words, losing weight as well as keeping the weight off is easier on a plant-based diet.

Benefit # 4 – Enhanced mood

The vegan diet is composed of foods that are rich in nutrients, such as unsaturated fats, omega-3 fatty acids, complex carbohydrates, and magnesium. These nutrients are necessary for proper brain function, including mood regulation.
Studies also suggest that microbes found in the gut affect mood and consuming fiber and probiotics as well as limiting the intake of animal fats and products help ensure that there is a high level of good bacteria in the gut.

Guidelines and Rules for Eating Vegan

There are no hard and fast rules for eating vegan. However, whether consciously or unconsciously, vegans often follow these guidelines in their food choices:

- Seasonality

Seasonal fruits and vegetables aren't just cheaper, they are also more nutritious and delicious as they are at their peak. Consuming produce that are in season also offers the bonus of being more environment friendly as these products are often found locally.

- Going for healthy fats

Good fats are generally found in seeds and nuts. These fats are considered healthy because they help in the absorption of other nutrients, as well as in aiding hormone production and formation of cell membranes. Healthy fats also help regulate genetic function.

- Boosting protein intake

The body needs protein to create and repair tissues and produce hormones and enzymes. Protein also makes up the blood, skin, muscles, cartilage, and bones, which is why it is important for any diet to contain enough protein to keep a person in good health. The most common plant-based sources of protein are beans, legumes, nuts, spirulina, and soy products, such as tofu, edamame, and tempeh, which are major components of most vegan diets.

- Loading up on fiber

Compared to their meat-eating counterparts, vegans consume more whole grains, nuts, seeds, legumes, as well as vegetables and fruits. Thus, they get a fair share of fiber from their diet.

- Supplementing

Despite eating a balanced diet, nutrient deficiency is common among vegans. Vitamin B12, for example, is usually lacking in the vegan diet because it is mostly found in animal sources like beef, organ meats, sardines, clams, tuna, and trout. For this reason, vegans are advised to take vitamin B12 supplements or consume more fortified foods.

What to Eat

Today, there are plenty of vegan ingredient alternatives that it's not too difficult to whip up some of the meal's vegans were used to eating before going on a completely plant-based diet.

Apart from fruits and vegetables, a typical vegan diet consists of:

- Tofu
- Tempeh
- Seitan
- Beans
- Lentils
- Seeds
- Nuts and nut milks
- Molasses and maple/rice syrup
- Ready-made vegan products like vegan meat, vegan cheese, plant-based yogurt, and others

What Not to Eat

All foods that originate from animals or contain animal products are on the do-not-eat list, such as:

- Beef
- Pork
- Chicken
- Fish
- Seafood

- Dairy
- Eggs
- Honey
- Foods that contain ingredients of animal origin, such as some wine and beer and certain chewing gums

Tips for Success

If you're already following a vegetarian diet, making the switch to an exclusively plant-based diet is much easier and has a higher chance of success. Thus, if animal products are part of most of your meals, try going vegetarian first.

You can then gradually replace eggs, dairy, and fish with vegan alternatives so the shift will be more manageable and sustainable.

The following are examples of other tips to help you successfully follow the vegan diet:

- Stock up on vegan staples, such as tofu, nuts, seeds, and vegan condiments.
- Apart from eating a balanced meal, make sure that you are getting enough of all the vital nutrients by taking supplements or consuming fortified foods.
- Find a group of like-minded individuals who can offer support and meal prep ideas. If you can't find vegans in your circle of friends, try checking online for social media groups or meetups that you can join.
- Many restaurants cater to people with various dietary requirements so eating out shouldn't be too difficult. However, you can always call ahead or check the establishment's website to make sure they have vegan options.
- To maximize the health benefits, you get from having a plant-based diet, it's necessary that you make the necessary lifestyle changes, such as exercising, getting adequate sleep, and managing stress.

- It's important to talk to your doctor if you have a health condition that may become aggravated by a sudden change in diet.
- Make meal planning and meal prep part of your routine.

Chapter 2: Why Meal Prep?

Benefits of Meal Prepping

Whether you are on a vegan diet or just want to get a head start on food prep for the week, there are many reasons why meal prepping should be part of your routine. No matter the reason, meal prep helps you:

Benefit # 1 - Save time

One of the biggest benefits of meal prepping is that you save time shopping and cooking for food during the week. While some meals don't take hours to cook, it can seem too much especially at the end of a very long day. When you know you have a meal ready to heat and/or eat, it relieves some of the stress and frees up time that you can use for something else.

Benefit # 2 - Save money

Buying food in bulk is a good way to save on grocery costs. Meal prepping also helps you avoid eating out too much, especially when you have no time to shop or cook food during the week.

Benefit # 3 - Save energy

Cooking a big batch of food at once uses up significantly less energy than cooking meals every single day.

Benefit # 4 - Reduce waste

Food waste is a huge problem in today's society, but one way to reduce the wastage of food is through meal prepping. When you plan your meals, you'll know how much food you need to cook and, therefore, you'll buy only the ingredients you need. Thus, you won't have stocks of food items that don't get used past their best before date. Moreover, because you buy food in bulk, you reduce the amount of food packaging that gets thrown away.

Benefit # 5 - Have control

Meal prepping gives you better control about what to eat and how much to eat, which is helpful if you are on a weight loss plan. For vegans, meal prep is important because you control the components of your meals and it helps ensure that you get enough of all the nutrients your body needs.

Benefit # 6 - Reduce your carbon footprint

Driving to and from the grocery and going to restaurants entail carbon emissions that you can reduce by shopping only once or twice a week.

The Common Mistakes by Meal Prepping Beginners

If you're new to meal prepping, the following are examples of common mistakes that you can avoid:

Mistake # 1 - Choosing the wrong recipes

Some meals are best eaten immediately so it's best to avoid these when doing your meal prep. Meals that can be fully or partially prepared in advance, easily reheated or thawed, or scaled up or down are excellent meal prepping recipes.

Mistake # 2 – Not having a strategy

Meal prepping can seem intimidating because it requires careful planning for efficient use of time and energy. However, once you get the hang of it meal prepping becomes more natural.

Something to remember no matter what kind of meal you are making is to take note of the length of the cooking time as well as the steps involved in the recipe.

Begin with the recipe that takes the longest to cook, look for opportunities for multitasking, and be organized in the use of kitchen appliance to minimize cleanup in between uses.

Mistake # 3 – Not setting aside enough time

Yes, meal prepping helps you save time but it's not something done magically. Obviously, it also takes time. If you don't set aside enough time for the food prep, cooking, and storing you'll end up so frustrated and overwhelmed you may never want to try doing it again. For starters, block off just an hour of the day to prep one or two recipes for the coming week. Then, gradually increase the time and the number of recipes to work on as you become more confident with the process.

Chapter 3: 30-Day Meal plan

Day 1

Breakfast: Avocado Pancakes

Lunch: Tomato Basil Pasta

Dinner: Tofu Shawarma Rice

Day 2

Breakfast: Pumpkin Oats

Lunch: Green Beans, Roasted Red Peppers and Onions

Dinner: Risotto with Tomato and Herbs

Day 3

Breakfast: Eggless Omelet

Lunch: Broccoli and Cauliflower in Lemon-Dill Sauce

Dinner: Vegetable Salad in Mason Jar

Day 4

Breakfast: Melon Muesli

Lunch: "Cheesy" Spinach Rolls

Dinner: Pesto Pasta

Day 5

Breakfast: Peanut Butter Toast with Apple Slices

Lunch: Vegan Tacos

Dinner: Edamame and Aleppo Pepper

Day 6

Breakfast: Oatmeal with Pears

Lunch: Grilled Broccoli with Chili Garlic Oil

Dinner: Steamed Cabbage and Carrots

Day 7

Breakfast: Hawaiian Toast

Lunch: Sushi Grain Meal

Dinner: Roasted Root Vegetables

Day 8

Breakfast: Thai Oatmeal

Lunch: Grilled Summer Veggies

Dinner: Quinoa and Snap Pea Salad

Day 9

Breakfast: Avocado and White Bean Toast

Lunch: Spinach with Walnuts & Avocado

Dinner: Lemon Garlic Broccoli

Day 10

Breakfast: Vegan Oatmeal Waffle

Lunch: Sweet Spicy Beans

Dinner: Mashed Potato with Carrots & Corn

Day 11

Breakfast: Tropical Oats

Lunch: Garlic Pea Shoots

Dinner: Roasted Vegetables in Balsamic Sauce

Day 12

Breakfast: Toast with Refried Beans

Lunch: Sauteed Green Beans, Mushrooms and Tomatoes

Dinner: Carrot and Radish Slaw with Sesame Dressing

Day 13

Breakfast: Tofu Omelet

Lunch: Grilled Barbecue Tofu

Dinner: Chickpea and Quinoa

Day 14

Breakfast: Vegan Banana Bread

Lunch: Roasted Vegetables in Balsamic Sauce

Dinner: Grilled Broccoli with Chili Garlic Oil

Day 15

Breakfast: Sweet Potato Hash Browns

Lunch: Lemon Mustard Baby Veggies

Dinner: Sauteed Green Beans, Mushrooms and Tomatoes

Day 16

Breakfast: Green Smoothie

Lunch: Beets, Edamame and Mixed Green Salad

Dinner: Roasted Veggies in Lemon Sauce

Day 17

Breakfast: Tomato, Mushroom and Spinach Quiche

Lunch: Collard Greens with Shiitake Mushrooms

Dinner: Vegan Tacos

Day 18

Breakfast: Apple, Pecans and Cinnamon Oatmeal

Lunch: Broccoli & Cauliflower in Lemon-Dill Sauce

Dinner: Superfood Buddha Bowl

Day 19

Breakfast: Vegan Breakfast Sandwich

Lunch: Black Bean and Corn Salad

Dinner: Burrito and Cauliflower Rice Bowl

Day 20

Breakfast: Cinnamon Quinoa

Lunch: Mashed Potato with Carrots and Corn

Dinner: Lemon Mustard Baby Veggies

Day 21

Breakfast: Pancakes with Strawberries

Lunch: Spicy Snow Pea and Tofu Stir Fry

Dinner: Veggie Kebabs

Day 22

Breakfast: Thai Oatmeal

Lunch: Black Beans with Rice

Dinner: Tomato Basil Pasta

Day 23

Breakfast: Peanut Butter Toast with Apple Slices

Lunch: Roasted Veggies in Lemon Sauce

Dinner: Spinach with Walnuts and Avocado

Day 24

Breakfast: Vegan French Toast

Lunch: Lemon Garlic Broccoli

Dinner: Veggie Kebabs

Day 25

Breakfast: Pumpkin Oats

Lunch: Burrito and Cauliflower Rice Bowl

Dinner: Mango with Quinoa and Black Beans

Day 26

Breakfast: Avocado Pancakes

Lunch: Carrot and Radish Slaw with Sesame Dressing

Dinner: Steamed Cabbage and Carrots

Day 27

Breakfast: Vegan Breakfast Taco

Lunch: Spicy Snow Pea and Tofu Stir Fry

Dinner: Superfood Buddha Bowl

Day 28

Breakfast: Granola Parfait

Lunch: Garlic Pea Shoots

Dinner: Grilled Summer Veggies

Day 29

Breakfast: Tapioca Porridge

Lunch: Tofu Shawarma Rice

Dinner: Risotto with Tomato & Herbs

Day 30

Breakfast: Banana and Nut Oatmeal

Lunch: Collard Greens with Shiitake Mushrooms

Dinner: Pesto Pasta

Chapter 4: Breakfast

Peanut Butter Toast with Apple Slices

Preparation Time: 5 minutes
Cooking Time: 0 minute
Serving: 1

Ingredients:

- 1 slice whole-wheat bread, toasted
- 2 tablespoons peanut butter
- ¼ cup apple, sliced
- ¼ teaspoon ground cardamom

Method:

1. Spread bread slice with peanut butter.
2. Top with apple slices and sprinkle with cardamom.
3. Store in a food container.

Nutritional Value:

- Calories 293
- Total Fat 17 g
- Saturated Fat 3 g
- Cholesterol 0 mg
- Sodium 204 mg
- Total Carbohydrate 21 g
- Dietary Fiber 5 g
- Total Sugars 5 g
- Protein 11 g
- Potassium 90 mg

Avocado Pancakes

Preparation Time: 15 minutes
Cooking Time: 10 minutes
Servings: 4

Ingredients:

- 2 tablespoons flaxseed meal
- 5 tablespoons water
- 1 cup almond milk (unsweetened)
- 2 tablespoons sugar
- 1 cup mashed ripe avocado
- 1 teaspoon vanilla extract
- ¼ teaspoon salt
- 1 teaspoon lemon zest
- 1 ½ teaspoons baking powder
- 1 cup all-purpose flour
- 1 teaspoon oil
- Blueberries

Method:

1. Put flaxseed meal in a bowl.
2. Stir in water.
3. Let sit for 5 minutes.
4. Add milk, sugar, avocado, vanilla extract, salt and lemon zest in a blender.
5. Blend until smooth.
6. Transfer mixture to a bowl and add the flaxseed mixture.
7. Stir in baking powder and flour.
8. In a pan over medium heat, add the oil.
9. Pour a small amount of the batter.
10. Flip once the surface starts to bubble.
11. Cook for 4 minutes per side.
12. Place in a food container and top with blueberries.

Nutritional Value:

- Calories 258
- Total Fat 7 g
- Saturated Fat 1 g
- Cholesterol 0 mg
- Sodium 374 mg

- Total Carbohydrate 43 g
- Dietary Fiber 8 g
- Total Sugars 7 g
- Protein 5 g
- Potassium 370 mg

Oatmeal with Pears

Preparation Time: 5 minutes
Cooking Time: 5 minutes
Serving: 1

Ingredients:

- ¼ cup rolled oats, cooked
- ¼ teaspoon ground ginger
- ¼ teaspoon ground cinnamon
- ¼ cup pear, sliced

Method:

1. Transfer cooked oats in a glass jar with lid.
2. Stir in the ginger and cinnamon.
3. Top with pear slices.

Nutritional Value:

- Calories 108
- Total Fat 2 g
- Saturated Fat 0 g
- Cholesterol 0 mg
- Sodium 5 mg
- Total Carbohydrate 21 g
- Dietary Fiber 3 g
- Total Sugars 4 g
- Protein 3 g
- Potassium 440 mg

Thai Oatmeal

Preparation Time: 10 minutes
Cooking Time: 5 minutes
Serving: 1

Ingredients:

- ½ cup rolled oats, cooked
- 1 tablespoon peanut butter
- ½ cup coconut milk (unsweetened)
- ½ teaspoon curry powder
- 1 teaspoon tamari
- 2 tablespoons tomatoes, chopped
- ¼ cup spinach, cooked and chopped
- 1 tablespoon cilantro, chopped

Method:

1. Place oats, peanut butter, milk, curry powder and tamari in a jar.
2. Mix well.
3. Refrigerate overnight.
4. Top with tomatoes, spinach and cilantro before serving.

Nutritional Value:

- Calories 307
- Total Fat 14 g
- Saturated Fat 4 g
- Cholesterol 0 mg
- Sodium 467 mg
- Total Carbohydrate 34 g
- Dietary Fiber 6 g
- Total Sugars 3 g
- Protein 10 g
- Potassium 294 mg

Tropical Oats

Preparation Time: 10 minutes
Cooking Time: 5 minutes
Serving: 1

Ingredients:

- ½ cup rolled oats, cooked
- ¾ cup coconut milk (unsweetened)
- 1 tablespoon dried mango, chopped
- ¼ cup pineapple, diced
- 1 ½ teaspoons chia seeds
- 1 ½ teaspoons shredded coconut (unsweetened)

Method:

1. Add layers of oats, coconut milk, mango, pineapple and chia seeds in a glass jar with lid.
2. Seal the jar and refrigerate until ready to eat.
3. Top with the coconut shreds before serving.

Nutritional Value:

- Calories 281
- Total Fat 10 g
- Saturated Fat 5 g
- Cholesterol 0 mg
- Sodium 147 mg
- Total Carbohydrate 42 g
- Dietary Fiber 8 g
- Total Sugars 10 g
- Protein 7 g
- Potassium 205 mg

Sweet Potato Hash Browns

Preparation Time: 10 minutes
Cooking Time: 6 minutes
Servings: 6

Ingredients:

- 1 clove garlic, grated
- ¼ cup shallot, chopped
- 5 cups sweet potato, shredded
- 3 tablespoons olive oil, divided
- Salt and pepper to taste

Method:

1. Put the garlic, shallot, sweet potato, 1 tablespoon olive oil, salt and pepper in a bowl.
2. Add 1 tablespoon oil in a pan over medium heat.
3. Pour a half cup of the sweet potato patty in the pan. Flatten using a spatula.
4. Cook the patty for 3 minutes per side.
5. Cook remaining patties with the remaining oil.

Nutritional Value:

- Calories 103
- Total Fat 7 g
- Saturated Fat 1 g
- Cholesterol 0 mg
- Sodium 208 mg
- Total Carbohydrate 9 g
- Dietary Fiber 1 g
- Total Sugars 3 g
- Protein 1 g
- Potassium 207 mg

Apple, Pecans & Cinnamon Oatmeal

Preparation Time: 5 minutes
Cooking Time: 10 minutes
Serving: 1

Ingredients:

- ½ cup rolled oats, cooked
- ½ tablespoon chia seeds
- 1 teaspoon maple syrup
- ¼ teaspoon ground cinnamon
- ½ cup (unsweetened) almond milk
- Salt to taste
- ½ cup apple, diced
- 2 tablespoons pecans, toasted

Method:

1. Layer the oats, maple syrup, cinnamon and almond milk in a glass jar.
2. Season with a little bit of salt.
3. Cover the jar and refrigerate.
4. Top with apples and pecans before serving.

Nutritional Value:

- Calories 215
- Total Fat 4 g
- Saturated Fat 1 g
- Cholesterol 0 mg
- Sodium 232 mg
- Total Carbohydrate 41 g
- Dietary Fiber 6 g
- Total Sugars 11 g
- Protein 6 g
- Potassium 249 mg

Pumpkin Oats

Preparation Time: 5 minutes
Cooking Time: 0 minute
Serving: 1

Ingredients:

- ½ cup rolled oats, cooked
- ½ cup soy milk
- 2 teaspoons maple syrup
- 3 tablespoons pumpkin puree
- ½ teaspoon vanilla extract
- ¼ teaspoon ground cinnamon
- Salt to taste
- Toasted pumpkin seeds

Method:

1. Mix the oats, soy milk, maple syrup, pumpkin puree, vanilla extract and cinnamon in a glass jar with lid.
2. Season with a pinch of salt.
3. Seal the jar and refrigerate.
4. Top with pumpkin seeds before serving.

Nutritional Value:

- Calories 182
- Total Fat 4 g
- Saturated Fat 1 g
- Cholesterol 0 mg
- Sodium 351 mg
- Total Carbohydrate 41 g
- Dietary Fiber 6 g
- Total Sugars 11 g
- Protein 6 g
- Potassium 290 mg

Hawaiian Toast

Preparation Time: 5 minutes
Cooking Time: 5 minutes
Serving: 1

Ingredients:

- 1 slice whole wheat bread, toasted
- 3 teaspoons tomato sauce
- 1 pineapple ring
- 3 teaspoons vegan cheese, shredded

Method:

1. Spread tomato sauce on the toast.
2. Pu the pineapple ring on top.
3. Top with shredded cheese.
4. Bake in the oven until the cheese has melted.
5. Store in a food container
6. Reheat before serving.

Nutritional Value:

- Calories 252
- Total Fat 11 g
- Saturated Fat 2 g
- Cholesterol 0 mg
- Sodium 230 mg
- Total Carbohydrate 33 g
- Dietary Fiber 5 g
- Total Sugars 8 g
- Protein 8 g
- Potassium 54 mg

Eggless Omelette

Preparation Time: 10 minutes
Cooking Time: 5 minutes
Servings: 2

Ingredients:

- 1 tablespoon olive oil
- 1 onion, sliced into strips
- 1 red bell pepper, sliced into strips
- 1 tomato, sliced into strips
- 4 servings vegan egg, beaten

Method:

1. Pour the oil in a pan over medium heat.
2. Add the onion, red bell pepper and tomato and cook for 2 to 3 minutes.
3. Transfer vegetables to a bowl.
4. Add the vegan eggs to the bowl.
5. Pour the mixture to the pan.
6. Cook for 3 minutes or until firm.
7. Store in a food container.
8. Reheat before serving.

Nutritional Value:

- Calories 107
- Total Fat 7.3g
- Saturated Fat 1g
- Cholesterol 0mg
- Sodium 5mg
- Total Carbohydrate 10.9g
- Dietary Fiber 2.4g
- Total Sugars 6.2g
- Protein 1.5g
- Potassium 266mg

Melon Muesli

Preparation Time: 10 minutes
Cooking Time: 5 minutes
Servings: 2

Ingredients:

- ½ cup muesli cereal (uncooked)
- ½ cup almond milk (unsweetened)
- ½ cup water
- ½ cup fresh cantaloupe, chopped
- 1 pinch ground cinnamon

Method:

1. In a heat proof bowl, mix the cereal, milk and water.
2. Microwave in high power for 5 minutes.
3. Top with the cantaloupe and season with cinnamon before serving.

Nutritional Value:

- Calories 96
- Total Fat 2 g
- Saturated Fat 0 g
- Cholesterol 0 mg
- Sodium 102 mg
- Total Carbohydrate 20 g
- Dietary Fiber 2 g
- Total Sugars 10 g
- Protein 3 g
- Potassium 259 mg

Avocado & White Bean Toast

Preparation Time: 5 minutes
Cooking Time: 0 minute
Serving: 1

Ingredients:

- ¼ avocado, mashed
- 1 slice whole-wheat bread, toasted
- ½ cup canned white beans, rinsed and drained
- Salt and pepper to taste

Method:

1. Spread mashed avocado on toasted bread.
2. Top with white beans.
3. Season with salt and pepper.

Nutritional Value:

- Calories 230
- Total Fat 9 g
- Saturated Fat 1 g
- Cholesterol 0 mg
- Sodium 459 mg
- Total Carbohydrate 35 g
- Dietary Fiber 11 g
- Total Sugars 3 g
- Protein 11 g
- Potassium 655 mg

Chapter 5: Lunch and Dinner

Veggie & Tofu Kebabs

Preparation Time: 15 minutes
Cooking Time: 12 minutes
Servings: 4

Ingredients:

- 2 cloves garlic, minced
- ¼ cup balsamic vinegar
- ¼ cup olive oil
- 1 tablespoon Italian seasoning
- Salt and pepper to taste
- 1 onion, sliced into quarters
- 12 medium mushrooms
- 16 cherry tomatoes
- 1 zucchini, sliced into rounds
- 1 cup tofu, cubed
- 4 cups cauliflower rice

Method:

1. In a bowl, mix the garlic, vinegar, oil, Italian seasoning, salt and pepper.
2. Toss the vegetable slices and tofu in the mixture.
3. Marinate for 1 hour.
4. Thread into 8 skewers and grill for 12 minutes, turning once or twice.
5. Add cauliflower rice into 4 food containers.
6. Add 2 kebab skewers on top of each container of cauliflower rice.
7. Reheat kebabs in the grill before serving.

Nutritional Value:

- Calories 58
- Total Fat 2 g
- Saturated Fat 0 g
- Cholesterol 0 mg

- Sodium 84 mg
- Total Carbohydrate 9 g
- Dietary Fiber 2 g

- Total Sugars 5 g
- Protein 2 g
- Potassium 509 mg

Carrot and Radish Slaw with Sesame Dressing

Preparation Time: 10 minutes
Cooking Time: 0 minute
Servings: 4

Ingredients:

- 2 tablespoons sesame oil, toasted
- 3 tablespoons rice vinegar
- ½ teaspoon sugar
- 2 tablespoons low sodium tamari
- 1 cup carrots, sliced into strips
- 2 cups radishes, sliced
- 2 tablespoons fresh cilantro, chopped
- 2 teaspoons sesame seeds, toasted

Method:

1. Mix the oil, vinegar, sugar and tamari in a bowl.
2. Add the carrots, radishes and cilantro.
3. Toss to coat evenly.
4. Let sit for 10 minutes.
5. Transfer to a food container.

Nutritional Value:

- Calories 98
- Total Fat 8 g
- Saturated Fat 1 g
- Cholesterol 0 mg
- Sodium 336 mg
- Total Carbohydrate 6 g
- Dietary Fiber 2 g
- Total Sugars 3 g
- Protein 2 g
- Potassium 241 mg

Spicy Snow Pea and Tofu Stir Fry

Preparation Time: 20 minutes
Cooking Time: 20 minutes
Servings: 4

Ingredients:

- 1 cup unsalted natural peanut butter
- 2 teaspoons brown sugar
- 2 tablespoons reduced-sodium soy sauce
- 2 teaspoons hot sauce
- 3 tablespoons rice vinegar
- 14 oz. tofu
- 4 teaspoons oil
- 1/4 cup onion, sliced
- 2 tablespoons ginger, grated
- 3 cloves garlic, minced
- 1/2 cup broccoli, sliced into florets
- 1/2 cup carrot, sliced into sticks
- 2 cups fresh snow peas, trimmed
- 2 tablespoons water
- 2 cups brown rice, cooked
- 4 tablespoons roasted peanuts (unsalted)

Method:

1. In a bowl, mix the peanut butter, sugar, soy sauce, hot sauce and rice vinegar.
2. Blend until smooth and set aside.
3. Drain the tofu and sliced into cubes.
4. Pat dry with paper towel.
5. Add oil to a pan over medium heat.
6. Add the tofu and cook for 2 minutes or until brown on all sides.
7. Transfer the tofu to a plate.
8. Add the onion, ginger and garlic to the pan.

9. Cook for 2 minutes.
10. Add the broccoli and carrot.
11. Cook for 5 minutes.
12. Stir in the snow peas.
13. Pour in the water and cover.
14. Cook for 4 minutes.
15. Add the peanut sauce to the pan along with the tofu.
16. Heat through for 30 seconds.
17. In a food container, add the brown rice and top with the tofu and vegetable stir fry.
18. Top with roasted peanuts.

Nutritional Value:

- Calories 514
- Total Fat 27 g
- Saturated Fat 4 g
- Cholesterol 0 mg
- Sodium 376 mg

- Total Carbohydrate 49 g
- Dietary Fiber 7 g
- Total Sugars 12 g
- Protein 22 g
- Potassium 319 mg

Roasted Veggies in Lemon Sauce

Preparation Time: 15 minutes
Cooking Time: 20 minutes
Servings: 5

Ingredients:

- 2 cloves garlic, sliced
- 1 ½ cups broccoli florets
- 1 ½ cups cauliflower florets
- 1 tablespoon olive oil
- Salt to taste
- 1 teaspoon dried oregano, crushed
- ¾ cup zucchini, diced
- ¾ cup red bell pepper, diced
- 2 teaspoons lemon zest

Method:

1. Preheat your oven to 425 degrees F.
2. In a baking pan, add the garlic, broccoli and cauliflower.
3. Toss in oil and season with salt and oregano.
4. Roast in the oven for 10 minutes.
5. Add the zucchini and bell pepper to the pan.
6. Stir well.
7. Roast for another 10 minutes.
8. Sprinkle lemon zest on top before serving.
9. Transfer to a food container and reheat before serving.

Nutritional Value:

- Calories 52
- Total Fat 3 g
- Saturated Fat 0 g
- Cholesterol 0 mg
- Sodium 134 mg
- Total Carbohydrate 5 g
- Dietary Fiber 2 g
- Total Sugars 2 g
- Protein 2 g
- Potassium 270 mg

Spinach with Walnuts & Avocado

Preparation Time: 5 minutes
Cooking Time: 0 minute
Servings: 1

Ingredients:

- 3 cups baby spinach
- ½ cup strawberries, sliced
- 1 tablespoon white onion, chopped
- 2 tablespoons vinaigrette
- ¼ medium avocado, diced
- 2 tablespoons walnut, toasted

Method:

1. Put the spinach, strawberries and onion in a glass jar with lid.
2. Drizzle dressing on top.
3. Top with avocado and walnuts.
4. Seal the lid and refrigerate until ready to serve.
5.
6. 296 calories; 18 g fat(2 g sat); 10 g fiber; 27 g carbohydrates; 8 g protein;
7. 63 mcg folate; 0 mg cholesterol; 11 g sugars; 0 g added sugars; 11,084 IU vitamin A; 103 mg
8. vitamin C; 192 mg calcium; 7 mg iron; 195 mg sodium; 385 mg

Nutritional Value:

- Calories 296
- Total Fat 18 g
- Saturated Fat 2 g
- Cholesterol 0 mg
- Sodium 195 mg
- Total Carbohydrate 27 g
- Dietary Fiber 10 g
- Total Sugars 11 g
- Protein 8 g
- Potassium 103 mg

Vegan Tacos

Preparation Time: 20 minutes
Cooking Time: 10 minutes
Servings: 4

Ingredients:

- ½ teaspoon onion powder
- ½ teaspoon garlic powder
- 1 teaspoon chili powder
- 2 tablespoons tamari
- 16 oz. tofu, drained and crumbled
- 1 tablespoon olive oil
- 1 ripe avocado
- 1 tablespoon vegan mayonnaise
- 1 teaspoon lime juice
- Salt to taste
- 8 corn tortillas, warmed
- ½ cup fresh salsa
- 2 cups iceberg lettuce, shredded
- Pickled radishes

Method:

1. Combine the onion powder, garlic powder, chili powder and tamari in a bowl.
2. Marinate the tofu in the mixture for 10 minutes.
3. Pour the oil in a pan over medium heat.
4. Cook the tofu mixture for 10 minutes.
5. In another bowl, mash the avocado and mix with mayo, lime juice and salt.
6. Stuff each corn tortilla with tofu mixture, mashed avocado, salsa and lettuce.
7. Serve with pickled radishes.

Nutritional Value:

- Calories 360
- Total Fat 21 g

- Saturated Fat 3 g
- Cholesterol 0 mg
- Sodium 610 mg
- Total Carbohydrate 33 g

- Dietary Fiber 8 g
- Total Sugars 4 g
- Protein 17 g
- Potassium 553 mg

Grilled Broccoli with Chili Garlic Oil

Preparation Time: 15 minutes
Cooking Time: 16 minutes
Servings: 4

Ingredients:

- 3 tablespoons olive oil, divided
- 2 tablespoons vegetable broth (unsalted)
- 2 cloves garlic, sliced thinly
- 1 chili pepper, julienned
- 1 1/2 lb. broccoli, sliced into florets
- Salt and pepper to taste
- 2 lemons, sliced in half

Method:

1. Preheat your grill to medium-high.
2. In a bowl, mix 1 tablespoon oil, garlic, broth and chili.
3. Heat in a pan over medium heat for 30 seconds.
4. In another bowl, toss the broccoli florets in salt, pepper and remaining oil.
5. Grill the broccoli florets for 10 minutes.
6. Grill the lemon slices for 5 minutes.
7. Toss the grilled broccoli and lemon in chili garlic oil.
8. Store in a food container and reheat before serving.

Nutritional Value:

- Calories 164
- Total Fat 11 g
- Saturated Fat 1 g
- Cholesterol 0 mg
- Sodium 208 mg
- Total Carbohydrate 12 g
- Dietary Fiber 2 g
- Total Sugars 4 g
- Protein 6 g
- Potassium 519 mg

Tomato Basil Pasta

Preparation Time: 5 minutes
Cooking Time: 10 minutes
Servings: 4

Ingredients:

- 2 cups low-sodium vegetable broth
- 2 cups water
- 8 oz. pasta
- 1 ½ teaspoons Italian seasoning
- 15 oz. canned diced tomatoes
- 2 tablespoons olive oil
- ½ teaspoon garlic powder
- ½ teaspoon onion powder
- ¼ teaspoon crushed red pepper
- ½ teaspoon salt
- 6 cups baby spinach
- ½ cup basil, chopped

Method:

1. Add all the ingredients except spinach and basil in a pot over high heat.
2. Mix well.
3. Cover the pot and bring to a boil.
4. Reduce the heat.
5. Simmer for 5 minutes.
6. Add the spinach and cook for 5 more minutes.
7. Stir in basil.
8. Transfer to a food container.
9. Microwave before serving.

Nutritional Value:

- Calories 339
- Total Fat 10 g

- Saturated Fat 1 g
- Cholesterol 0 mg
- Sodium 465 mg
- Total Carbohydrate 55 g

- Dietary Fiber 8 g
- Total Sugars 6 g
- Protein 11 g
- Potassium 308 mg

Risotto with Tomato & Herbs

Preparation Time: 10 minutes
Cooking Time: 20 minutes
Servings: 32

Ingredients:

- 2 oz. Arborio rice
- 1 teaspoon dried garlic, minced
- 3 tablespoons dried onion, minced
- 1 tablespoon dried Italian seasoning, crushed
- ¾ cup snipped dried tomatoes
- 1 ½ cups reduced-sodium chicken broth

Method:

1. Make the dry risotto mix by combining all the ingredients except broth in a large bowl.
2. Divide the mixture into eight resealable plastic bags. Seal the bag.
3. Store at room temperature for up to 3 months.
4. When ready to serve, pour the broth in a pot.
5. Add the contents of 1 plastic bag of dry risotto mix.
6. Bring to a boil and then reduce heat.
7. Cover the pot and simmer for 20 minutes.
8. Serve with vegetables.

Nutritional Value:

- Calories 80
- Total Fat 0 g
- Saturated Fat 0 g
- Cholesterol 0 mg
- Sodium 276 mg
- Total Carbohydrate 17 g
- Dietary Fiber 2 g
- Total Sugars 0 g
- Protein 3 g
- Potassium 320 mg

Tofu Shawarma Rice

Preparation Time: 15 minutes
Cooking Time: 15 minutes
Servings: 4

Ingredients:

- 4 cups cooked brown rice
- 4 cups cooked tofu, sliced into small cubes
- 4 cups cucumber, cubed
- 4 cups tomatoes, cubed
- 4 cups white onion, cubed
- 2 cups cabbage, shredded
- 1/2 cup vegan mayo
- 1/8 cup garlic, minced
- Garlic salt to taste
- Hot sauce

Method:

1. Add brown rice into 4 food containers.
2. Arrange tofu, cucumber, tomatoes, white onion and cabbage on top.
3. In a bowl, mix the mayo, garlic, and garlic salt.
4. Drizzle top with garlic sauce and hot sauce before serving.

Nutritional Value:

- Calories 667
- Total Fat 12.6g
- Saturated Fat 2.2g
- Cholesterol 0mg
- Sodium 95mg
- Total Carbohydrate 116.5g
- Dietary Fiber 9.9g
- Total Sugars 9.4g
- Protein 26.1g
- Potassium 1138mg

Pesto Pasta

Preparation Time: 10 minutes
Cooking Time: 8 minutes
Servings: 2

Ingredients:

- 1 cup fresh basil leaves
- 4 cloves garlic
- 2 tablespoons walnut
- 2 tablespoons olive oil
- 1 tablespoon vegan Parmesan cheese
- 2 cups cooked penne pasta
- 2 tablespoons black olives, sliced

Method:

1. Put the basil leaves, garlic, walnut, olive oil and Parmesan cheese in a food processor.
2. Pulse until smooth.
3. Divide pasta into 2 food containers.
4. Spread the basil sauce on top.
5. Top with black olives.
6. Store until ready to serve.

Nutritional Value:

- Calories 374
- Total Fat 21.1g
- Saturated Fat 2.6g
- Cholesterol 47mg
- Sodium 92mg
- Total Carbohydrate 38.6g
- Dietary Fiber 1.1g
- Total Sugars 0.2g
- Protein 10g
- Potassium 215mg

"Cheesy" Spinach Rolls

Preparation Time: 20 minutes
Cooking Time: 15 minutes
Servings: 6

Ingredients:

- 18 spinach leaves
- 18 vegan spring roll wrappers
- 6 slices cheese, cut into 18 smaller strips
- Water
- 1 cup vegetable oil
- 6 cups cauliflower rice
- 3 cups tomato, cubed
- 3 cups cucumber, cubed
- 1 tablespoon olive oil
- 1 teaspoon balsamic vinegar

Method:

1. Place one spinach leaf on top of each wrapper.
2. Add a small strip of vegan cheese on top of each spinach leaf.
3. Roll the wrapper and seal the edges with water.
4. In a pan over medium high heat, add the vegetable oil.
5. Cook the rolls until golden brown.
6. Drain in paper towels.
7. Divide cauliflower rice into 6 food containers.
8. Add 3 cheesy spinach rolls in each food container.
9. Toss cucumber and tomato in olive oil and vinegar.
10. Place the cucumber tomato relish beside the rolls.
11. Seal and reheat in the microwave when ready to serve.

Nutritional Value:

- Calories 746
- Total Fat 38.5g

- Saturated Fat 10.1g
- Cholesterol 33mg
- Sodium 557mg
- Total Carbohydrate 86.2g
- Dietary Fiber 3.8g
- Total Sugars 2.6g
- Protein 18g
- Potassium 364mg

Grilled Summer Veggies

Preparation Time: 15 minutes
Cooking Time: 6 minutes
Servings: 6

Ingredients:

- 2 teaspoons cider vinegar
- 1 tablespoon olive oil
- ¼ teaspoon fresh thyme, chopped
- 1 teaspoon fresh parsley, chopped
- ¼ teaspoon fresh rosemary, chopped
- Salt and pepper to taste
- 1 onion, sliced into wedges
- 2 red bell peppers, sliced
- 3 tomatoes, sliced in half
- 6 large mushrooms, stems removed
- 1 eggplant, sliced crosswise
- 3 tablespoons olive oil
- 1 tablespoon cider vinegar

Method:

1. Make the dressing by mixing the vinegar, oil, thyme, parsley, rosemary, salt and pepper.
2. In a bowl, mix the onion, red bell pepper, tomatoes, mushrooms and eggplant.
3. Toss in remaining olive oil and cider vinegar.
4. Grill over medium heat for 3 minutes.
5. Turn the vegetables and grill for another 3 minutes.
6. Arrange grilled vegetables in a food container.
7. Drizzle with the herbed mixture when ready to serve.

Nutritional Value:

- Calories 127
- Total Fat 9 g

- Saturated Fat 1 g
- Cholesterol 0 mg
- Sodium 55 mg
- Total Carbohydrate 11 g

- Dietary Fiber 5 g
- Total Sugars 5 g
- Protein 3 g
- Potassium 464 mg

Superfood Buddha Bowl

Preparation Time: 10 minutes
Cooking Time: 10 minutes
Servings: 4

Ingredients:

- 8 oz. microwavable quinoa
- 2 tablespoons lemon juice
- ½ cup hummus
- Water
- 5 oz. baby kale
- 8 oz. cooked baby beets, sliced
- 1 cup frozen shelled edamame (thawed)
- ¼ cup sunflower seeds, toasted
- 1 avocado, sliced
- 1 cup pecans
- 2 tablespoons flaxseeds

Method:

1. Cook quinoa according to directions in the packaging.
2. Set aside and let cool.
3. In a bowl, mix the lemon juice and hummus.
4. Add water to achieve desired consistency.
5. Divide mixture into 4 condiment containers.
6. Cover containers with lids and put in the refrigerator.
7. Divide the baby kale into 4 food containers with lids.
8. Top with quinoa, beets, edamame and sunflower seeds.
9. Store in the refrigerator until ready to serve.
10. Before serving add avocado slices and hummus dressing.

Nutritional Value:

- Calories 381
- Total Fat 19 g

- Saturated Fat 2 g
- Cholesterol 0 mg
- Sodium 188 mg
- Total Carbohydrate 43 g

- Dietary Fiber 13 g
- Total Sugars 8 g
- Protein 16 g
- Potassium 1,066 mg

Burrito & Cauliflower Rice Bowl

Preparation Time: 15 minutes
Cooking Time: 10 minutes
Servings: 4

Ingredients:

- 1 cup cooked tofu cubes
- 12 oz. frozen cauliflower rice
- 4 teaspoons olive oil
- 1 teaspoon unsalted taco seasoning
- 1 cup red cabbage, sliced thinly
- ½ cup salsa
- ¼ cup fresh cilantro, chopped
- 1 cup avocado, diced

Method:

1. Prepare cauliflower rice according to directions in the package.
2. Toss cauliflower rice in olive oil and taco seasoning.
3. Divide among 4 food containers with lid.
4. Top with tofu, cabbage, salsa and cilantro.
5. Seal the container and chill in the refrigerator until ready to serve.
6. Before serving, add avocado slices.

Nutritional Value:

- Calories 298
- Total Fat 20 g
- Saturated Fat 3 g
- Cholesterol 0 mg
- Sodium 680 mg
- Total Carbohydrate 15 g
- Dietary Fiber 6 g
- Total Sugars 5 g
- Protein 15 g
- Potassium 241 mg

Chapter 6: Vegetables

Lemon Garlic Broccoli

Preparation Time: 10 minutes
Cooking Time: 10 minutes
Servings: 2

Ingredients:

- 2 teaspoons olive oil
- 3 cloves garlic, minced
- 2 cups broccoli, sliced into florets
- Salt and pepper to taste
- 1 tablespoon freshly squeezed lemon juice

Method:

1. In a pan over medium heat, pour the olive oil.
2. Once hot, add the garlic and cook for 30 seconds.
3. Add the broccoli florets and cook until tender
4. Stir in the lemon juice. Let cool.
5. Put in a food container and reheat when ready to eat.

Nutritional Value:

- Calories 80
- Total Fat 5.1g
- Saturated Fat 0.7g
- Cholesterol 0mg
- Sodium 32mg
- Total Carbohydrate 7.7g
- Dietary Fiber 2.5g
- Total Sugars 1.8g
- Protein 2.9g
- Potassium 316mg

Steamed Cabbage & Carrots

Preparation Time: 10 minutes
Cooking Time: 20 minutes
Servings: 8

Ingredients:

- 2 teaspoons olive oil
- 1 cup carrots, sliced
- 1 green bell pepper, sliced into strips
- 1 head green cabbage, sliced
- 2 tablespoons water
- Salt and pepper to taste

Method:

1. Pour oil in a pot over medium heat.
2. Add carrot strips and cook for 5 minutes.
3. Add bell pepper and cabbage.
4. Pour in the water and season with salt and pepper.
5. Cover the pot.
6. Cook for 15 minutes or until tender.
7. Store in food container and reheat when ready to eat.

Nutritional Value:

- Calories 36
- Total Fat 1 g
- Saturated Fat 0 g
- Cholesterol 0 mg
- Sodium 168 mg
- Total Carbohydrate 6 g
- Dietary Fiber 2 g
- Total Sugars 3 g
- Protein 1 g
- Potassium 226 mg

Collard Greens with Shiitake Mushrooms

Preparation Time: 15 minutes
Cooking Time: 10 minutes
Servings: 4

Ingredients:

- ¼ teaspoon salt
- ¾ teaspoon smoked paprika
- ¼ teaspoon red pepper, crushed
- ¼ teaspoon ground cumin
- ¾ cup reduced-sodium vegetable broth
- 2 tablespoons olive oil
- 4 cloves garlic, minced
- 5 oz. shiitake mushrooms, chopped
- 16 oz. collard greens, chopped
- 2 tablespoons cider vinegar
- 1 teaspoon hot sauce
- ½ teaspoon ground pepper

Method:

1. Add salt, paprika, red pepper, cumin and broth in a pan over medium heat.
2. Simmer for 1 minute, stirring to blend well.
3. Transfer to a plate and set aside.
4. In a pot over medium high heat, add the oil.
5. Cook the garlic and mushrooms for 4 minutes.
6. Pour 2 tablespoons of the paprika mixture to the pot.
7. Mix well.
8. Add the collard greens and gradually add the remaining paprika mixture.
9. Stir in the rest of the ingredients.
10. Cook for 1 minute.
11. Store in a food container and reheat when ready to eat.

Nutritional Value:

- Calories 120
- Total Fat 8 g

- Saturated Fat 1 g
- Cholesterol 0 mg
- Sodium 227 mg
- Total Carbohydrate 11 g

- Dietary Fiber 6 g
- Total Sugars 2 g
- Protein 5 g
- Potassium 384 mg

Garlic Pea Shoots

Preparation Time: 5 minutes
Cooking Time: 5 minutes
Servings: 6

Ingredients:

- 2 tablespoons canola oil
- 2 tablespoons sesame oil
- 3 tablespoons garlic, minced
- 1 lb. pea shoots
- ¼ cup rice wine
- Salt and pepper to taste

Method:

1. Heat both of the oils in a pot over medium high heat.
2. Add garlic and cook for 30 seconds, stirring frequently.
3. Add pea shoots and rice wine.
4. Season with salt and pepper.
5. Cook for 3 minutes.
6. Place in a food container and heat in the microwave when ready to eat.

Nutritional Value:

- Calories 150
- Total Fat 10 g
- Saturated Fat 1 g
- Cholesterol 0 mg
- Sodium 291 mg
- Total Carbohydrate 7 g
- Dietary Fiber 2 g
- Total Sugars 3 g
- Protein 2 g
- Potassium 3 mg

Mashed Potato with Carrots & Corn

Preparation Time: 15 minutes
Cooking Time: 30 minutes
Servings: 4

Ingredients:

- Water
- 8 potatoes, peeled and cubed
- Salt
- 4 tablespoons vegan butter, divided
- 1 cup frozen corn and carrot cubes
- Salt and pepper to taste
- 1 cup pecans
- 2 tablespoons flaxseeds

Method:

1. Fill a pot with water.
2. Put in the stove and bring to a boil.
3. Add the potatoes.
4. Simmer until the potatoes are tender.
5. Take the potatoes out of the pot and drain.
6. Mash the potatoes using a fork or a masher.
7. Stir in 3 tablespoons butter.
8. Season with salt and pepper.
9. In a pan over medium heat, add remaining butter.
10. Add the frozen vegetables.
11. Sauté for 3 minutes.
12. Drain the liquid.
13. Divide the mashed potato in food containers.
14. Top with the cubed corn and carrots.
15. Reheat before serving.

Nutritional Value:

- Calories 556
- Total Fat 26.5g

- Saturated Fat 2.8g
- Cholesterol 0mg
- Sodium 65mg
- Total Carbohydrate 72.9g

- Dietary Fiber 14.9g
- Total Sugars 6.2g
- Protein 11.6g
- Potassium 1908mg

Sautéed Green Beans, Mushrooms & Tomatoes

Preparation Time: 15 minutes
Cooking Time: 15 minutes
Servings: 10

Ingredients:

- Water
- 3 lb. green beans, trimmed
- 2 tablespoons olive oil
- 8 cloves garlic, minced
- ½ cup tomato, diced
- 12 oz. cremini mushrooms, sliced into quarters
- Salt and pepper to taste

Method:

1. Fill a pot with water.
2. Bring to a boil.
3. Add the beans and cook for 5 minutes.
4. Drain the beans.
5. Dry the pot.
6. Pour oil into the pot.
7. Add garlic, tomato and mushrooms.
8. Cook for 5 minutes.
9. Add the beans and cook for another 5 minutes.
10. Season with salt and pepper.
11. Store in a food container and reheat before eating.

Nutritional Value:

- Calories 74
- Total Fat 3 g
- Saturated Fat 0 g
- Cholesterol 0 mg
- Sodium 185 mg
- Total Carbohydrate 11 g
- Dietary Fiber 4 g
- Total Sugars 5 g
- Protein 3 g
- Potassium 438 mg

Lemon Mustard Baby Veggies

Preparation Time: 15 minutes
Cooking Time: 10 minutes
Servings: 8

Ingredients:

- 1 clove garlic, minced
- 2 tablespoons fresh lemon juice
- 1 teaspoon Dijon mustard
- 2 tablespoons olive oil, divided
- 2 tablespoons water
- ½ teaspoon lemon zest
- 2 teaspoons fresh basil, chopped
- 1 lb. baby zucchini
- ½ lb. baby carrots
- ½ lb. baby potatoes
- 12 cherry tomatoes

Method:

1. Mix garlic, lemon juice, mustard, half of olive oil, water and lemon zest in a bowl.
2. Transfer to a glass jar with lid.
3. Pour remaining olive oil in a pan over medium heat.
4. Once hot, add the vegetables.
5. Cook until tender.
6. Drain and transfer in a food container.
7. When ready to eat, reheat veggies and toss in the lemon mustard sauce.

Nutritional Value:

- Calories 57
- Total Fat 2 g
- Saturated Fat 0 g
- Cholesterol 0 mg
- Sodium 190 mg
- Total Carbohydrate 9 g
- Dietary Fiber 3 g
- Total Sugars 5 g
- Protein 2 g
- Potassium 343 mg

Roasted Vegetables in Balsamic Sauce

Preparation Time: 10 minutes
Cooking Time: 23 minutes
Servings: 12

Ingredients:

- 1 onion, sliced into wedges
- 2 cloves garlic, minced
- 1 lb. green beans, trimmed
- 2 tablespoons olive oil
- Salt and pepper to taste
- 4 yellow summer squash, sliced
- ⅔ cup balsamic vinegar

Method:

1. Preheat your oven to 450 degrees F.
2. Toss onion, garlic and beans in olive oil.
3. Transfer to a baking pan.
4. Season with salt and pepper.
5. Roast in the oven for 8 minutes.
6. Add the squash.
7. Roast for another 5 minutes.
8. In a pan over medium high heat, pour the balsamic vinegar and bring to a boil.
9. Reduce heat and simmer for 10 minutes.
10. Transfer roasted vegetables in a food container.
11. Reheat the veggies and toss in balsamic vinegar sauce when ready to serve.

Nutritional Value:

- Calories 90
- Total Fat 4 g
- Saturated Fat 1 g
- Cholesterol 0 mg
- Sodium 45 mg
- Total Carbohydrate 13 g
- Dietary Fiber 3 g
- Total Sugars 9 g
- Protein 2 g
- Potassium 45 mg

Roasted Root Vegetables

Preparation Time: 20 minutes
Cooking Time: 1 hour and 10 minutes
Servings: 8

Ingredients:

- 2 cups celery root, sliced
- 1 ½ cups baby carrots, peeled
- 8 oz. baby potatoes, sliced in half
- 3 parsnips, sliced
- 1 fennel bulb, cored and quartered
- 2 shallots, sliced
- 2 tablespoons olive oil
- Salt and pepper to taste

Method:

1. Preheat your oven to 325 degrees F.
2. In a baking pan, put all the root vegetables and toss to combine.
3. Drizzle with oil and season with salt and pepper.
4. Mix well.
5. Bake for 1 hour.
6. Increase temperature of your oven to 425 degrees F.
7. Bake for 10 minutes.
8. Transfer to a food container.
9. Reheat in pan without oil before serving.

Nutritional Value:

- Calories 82
- Total Fat 2 g
- Saturated Fat 0 g
- Cholesterol 0 mg
- Sodium 136 mg
- Total Carbohydrate 14 g
- Dietary Fiber 3 g
- Total Sugars 4 g
- Protein 2 g
- Potassium 407 mg

Green Beans, Roasted Red Peppers & Onions

Preparation Time: 15 minutes
Cooking Time: 25 minutes
Servings: 6

Ingredients:

- 1 tablespoon olive oil
- 1 ½ cups onion, chopped
- 1 tablespoon red wine vinegar
- ½ cup jarred roasted red peppers, drained and chopped
- 2 tablespoons fresh basil, chopped
- ¼ cup olives, pitted and sliced
- Salt and pepper to taste
- 1 lb. fresh green beans, trimmed and sliced

Method:

1. Pour olive oil in a pan over medium heat.
2. Add onion and cook for 10 minutes.
3. Pour in the vinegar.
4. Cook for 2 minutes.
5. Add roasted red peppers, basil and olives.
6. Season with salt and pepper.
7. Remove from the stove.
8. In a saucepan with water, cook beans for 10 minutes.
9. Add beans to the onion mixture.
10. Stir for 3 minutes.

Nutritional Value:

- Calories 73
- Total Fat 3 g
- Saturated Fat 0 g
- Cholesterol 0 mg
- Sodium 153 mg
- Total Carbohydrate 11 g
- Dietary Fiber 4 g
- Total Sugars 3 g
- Protein 2 g
- Potassium 248 mg

Broccoli & Cauliflower in Lemon-Dill Sauce

Preparation Time: 10 minutes
Cooking Time: 20 minutes
Servings: 4

Ingredients:

- 1 tablespoon olive oil
- 2 teaspoons lemon juice
- ½ teaspoon dried dill weed
- 1 clove garlic, minced
- Salt and pepper to taste
- ⅛ teaspoon dry mustard
- 2 cups cauliflower florets
- 2 cups broccoli florets
- Fresh dill sprigs

Method:

1. Preheat your oven to 375 degrees F.
2. Add olive oil, lemon juice, dill, garlic, salt, pepper and mustard in a glass jar with lid.
3. Shake to blend well.
4. In a baking pan, toss cauliflower and broccoli in 3 tablespoons lemon dill sauce.
5. Bake in the oven for 20 minutes or until tender.
6. Toss in the remaining sauce before serving.

Nutritional Value:

- Calories 60
- Total Fat 4 g
- Saturated Fat 1 g
- Cholesterol 0 mg
- Sodium 103 mg
- Total Carbohydrate 6 g
- Dietary Fiber 2 g
- Total Sugars 2 g
- Protein 2 g
- Potassium 301 mg

Vegetable Salad in Mason Jar

Preparation Time: 5 minutes
Cooking Time: 0 minute
Servings: 1

Ingredients:

- 2 tablespoons cashew sauce (recipe in the sauce section)
- 1 cup tofu cubes, roasted
- 1 tablespoon pumpkin seeds
- 1 cup carrots, roasted
- 2 cups mixed greens

Method:

1. In a glass jar, layer the cashew sauce, tofu, seeds, carrots and mixed greens.
2. Seal the jar.
3. Refrigerate up to 5 days.
4. Serve whenever ready to eat.

Nutritional Value:

- Calories 400
- Total Fat 27 g
- Saturated Fat 5 g
- Cholesterol 0 mg
- Sodium 383 mg
- Total Carbohydrate 21 g
- Dietary Fiber 8 g
- Total Sugars 5 g
- Protein 27 g
- Potassium 895 mg

Chapter 7: Grain and Bean

Sweet Spicy Beans

Preparation Time: 10 minutes
Cooking Time: 50 minutes
Servings: 10

Ingredients:

- 3 tablespoons vegetable oil
- 1 onion, chopped
- 45 oz. navy beans, rinsed and drained
- 1 ½ cups water
- ¾ cup ketchup
- ⅓ cup brown sugar
- 1 tablespoon white vinegar
- 1 teaspoon chipotle peppers in adobo sauce
- Salt and pepper to taste

Method:

1. Pour the oil in a pan over medium heat.
2. Add onion and cook for 10 minutes.
3. Add the rest of the ingredients.
4. Bring to a boil.
5. Reduce heat and simmer for 30 minutes.
6. Transfer to food container.
7. Reheat when ready to eat.

Nutritional Value:

- Calories 191
- Total Fat 4 g
- Saturated Fat 0 g
- Cholesterol 0 mg
- Sodium 354 mg
- Total Carbohydrate 32 g
- Dietary Fiber 7 g
- Total Sugars 12 g
- Protein 7 g
- Potassium 361 mg

Edamame & Aleppo Pepper

Preparation Time: 5 minutes
Cooking Time: 5 minutes
Serving: 1

Ingredients:

- ½ cup edamame pods
- Water
- ⅛ teaspoon Aleppo pepper

Method:

1. Place edamame pods in a steamer basket.
2. Put the basket on top of a pot with water.
3. Steam.
4. Store in glass jar with lid.
5. Season with Aleppo pepper before serving.

Nutritional Value:

- Calories 101
- Total Fat 3 g
- Saturated Fat 0 g
- Cholesterol 0 mg
- Sodium 30 mg
- Total Carbohydrate 9 g
- Dietary Fiber 4 g
- Total Sugars 1 g
- Protein 8 g
- Potassium 4 mg

Sushi Grain Meal

Preparation Time: 20 minutes
Cooking Time: 0 minute
Servings: 4

Ingredients:

- 2 teaspoons fresh ginger, grated
- 2 tablespoons low sodium tamari
- 2 tablespoons rice vinegar
- 2 teaspoons sesame oil, toasted
- 2 tablespoons avocado oil
- 2 cups brown rice, cooked
- 1 cup cucumber, diced
- 1 cup carrot, shredded
- 1 avocado, diced
- 1 cup toasted nori, chopped
- 1 cup shelled edamame, cooked
- Sesame seeds

Method:

1. In a bowl, mix the ginger, tamari, vinegar, sesame oil and avocado oil.
2. Divide brown rice among 4 food containers with lids.
3. Top with the cucumber, carrot, avocado, nori and edamame.
4. Sprinkle sesame seeds on top.
5. Seal the container and refrigerate.
6. Drizzle sauce on top when ready to eat.

Nutritional Value:

- Calories 341
- Total Fat 20 g
- Saturated Fat 3 g
- Cholesterol 0 mg
- Sodium 381 mg
- Total Carbohydrate 35 g
- Dietary Fiber 8 g
- Total Sugars 3 g
- Protein 20 g
- Potassium 596 mg

Quinoa & Snap Pea Salad

Preparation Time: 20 minutes
Cooking Time: 20 minutes
Servings: 6

Ingredients:

- 2 cups water
- 1 cup quinoa
- ⅓ cup onion, sliced
- 1 ½ cups mushrooms, sliced
- 1 tablespoon fresh dill, chopped
- 2 cups fresh snap peas, trimmed and sliced
- ⅓ cup white wine vinegar
- ¼ cup flaxseed oil
- 1 teaspoon lemon zest
- 1 tablespoon lemon juice
- 1 teaspoon maple syrup

Method:

1. Put quinoa and water in a pan over medium high heat.
2. Bring to a boil.
3. Reduce heat and simmer for 15 minutes.
4. Fluff using a fork and set aside.
5. In a bowl, combine onion, mushrooms, dill and peas.
6. In another bowl, mix the rest of the ingredients.
7. Transfer the quinoa in a food container.
8. Stir in the pea mixture.
9. Seal the container and refrigerate until ready to serve.
10. Transfer the maple dressing into a glass jar with lid.
11. Drizzle dressing over the quinoa salad before serving.

Nutritional Value:

- Calories 223
- Total Fat 11 g
- Saturated Fat 2 g
- Cholesterol 0 mg

- Sodium 10 mg
- Total Carbohydrate 25 g
- Dietary Fiber 3 g
- Total Sugars 6 g
- Protein 6 g
- Potassium 311 mg

Chickpea & Quinoa

Preparation Time: 15 minutes
Cooking Time: 0 minute
Serving: 1

Ingredients:

- 3 tablespoons hummus
- 1 tablespoon lemon juice
- 1 tablespoon roasted red pepper, chopped
- 1 tablespoon water
- Salt and pepper to taste
- 1 cup cooked quinoa
- ¼ avocado, diced
- ⅓ cup canned chickpeas, rinsed and drained
- ½ cup cherry tomatoes, sliced in half
- ½ cup cucumber, sliced

Method:

1. In a glass jar with lid, mix the hummus, lemon juice, red pepper, water, salt and pepper.
2. Shake to mix.
3. Arrange the rest of the ingredients in a food container.
4. Drizzle with sauce when ready to eat.

Nutritional Value:

- Calories 503
- Total Fat 17 g
- Saturated Fat 2 g
- Cholesterol 0 mg
- Sodium 573 mg
- Total Carbohydrate 75 g
- Dietary Fiber 16 g
- Total Sugars 6 g
- Protein 18 g
- Potassium 1,083 mg

Beets, Edamame & Mixed Green Salad

Preparation Time: 10 minutes
Cooking Time: 0 minute
Serving: 1

Ingredients:

- 2 cups mixed greens
- ½ raw beet, peeled and shredded
- 1 cup shelled edamame, thawed
- 1 tablespoon red wine vinegar
- 1 tablespoon fresh cilantro, chopped
- 2 teaspoons extra-virgin olive oil
- Pepper to taste

Method:

1. Place the mixed greens in a food container.
2. Top with shredded beets and edamame.
3. In a glass jar with lid, mix the rest of the ingredients.
4. Refrigerate the salad and drizzle with the dressing when ready to eat.

Nutritional Value:

- Calories 325
- Total Fat 16 g
- Saturated Fat 1 g
- Cholesterol 0 mg
- Sodium 682 mg
- Total Carbohydrate 25 g
- Dietary Fiber 12 g
- Total Sugars 6 g
- Protein 18 g
- Potassium 499 mg

Black Bean & Corn Salad

Preparation Time: 15 minutes
Cooking Time: 0 minute
Servings: 4

Ingredients:

- 2 tablespoons olive oil
- ¼ cup lime juice
- ¼ cup fresh cilantro, chopped
- Salt and pepper to taste
- 2 cups red cabbage, shredded
- 2 ¼ cups corn kernels
- ⅓ cup pine nuts, toasted
- 30 oz. canned black beans, rinsed and drained
- 1 tomato, diced
- ½ cup red onion, minced

Method:

1. In a glass jar with lid, blend the oil, lime juice, cilantro, salt and pepper.
2. In a food container, arrange the red cabbage, topped with the rest of the ingredients.
3. Cover and refrigerate until ready to serve.
4. Drizzle with dressing before serving.

Nutritional Value:

- Calories 415
- Total Fat 16 g
- Saturated Fat 2 g
- Cholesterol 0 mg
- Sodium 480 mg
- Total Carbohydrate 58 g
- Dietary Fiber 14 g
- Total Sugars 16 g
- Protein 16 g
- Potassium 1,112 mg

Black Beans with Rice

Preparation Time: 20 minutes
Cooking Time: 2 hours and 15 minutes
Servings: 8

Ingredients:

- 1 lb. dried black beans, soaked in water overnight, rinsed and drained
- 8 cups water, divided
- 2 tablespoons dried oregano
- 1 bay leaf
- 6 cloves garlic, crushed
- 2 teaspoons olive oil
- 1 onion, chopped
- 1 red bell pepper, chopped
- 1 tablespoon ground cumin
- 1 jalapeño pepper, chopped
- 2 tablespoons balsamic vinegar
- Salt and pepper to taste
- 2 cups long-grain white rice
- 8 lime wedges

Method:

1. Put black beans in a pot.
2. Add 4 cups water, oregano, bay leaf and garlic.
3. Bring to a boil.
4. Reduce heat and simmer for 2 hours.
5. Drain and put beans back to the pot.
6. Pour in the oil.
7. Add onion and bell pepper. Cook for 5 minutes.
8. Add jalapeño pepper and cumin. Cook for 1 minute.
9. Season with salt and pepper.
10. In another saucepan, add remaining water and salt.

11. Add rice and cover.
12. Bring to a boil and then simmer for 15 minutes.
13. Put rice in a food container and top with beans.
14. Garnish with lemon wedges.
15. Refrigerate and then reheat before serving.

Nutritional Value:

- Calories 600
- Total Fat 2 g
- Saturated Fat 0 g
- Cholesterol 0 mg
- Sodium 407 mg

- Total Carbohydrate 117 g
- Dietary Fiber 11 g
- Total Sugars 7 g
- Protein 24 g
- Potassium 230 mg

Slow Cooked Beans

Preparation Time: 10 minutes
Cooking Time: 2 hours and 15 minutes
Servings: 4

Ingredients:

- 1 lb. black beans, soaked overnight, rinsed and drained
- 1 onion, chopped
- 1 bay leaf
- 4 cloves garlic, minced
- 1 teaspoon dried thyme
- 5 cups boiling water
- Salt to taste

Method:

1. Add the beans to a slow cooker.
2. Stir in onion, bay leaf, garlic and thyme.
3. Add water and cover the pot.
4. Cook for 2 hours.
5. Season with salt and cook for another 15 minutes.

Nutritional Value:

- Calories 253
- Total Fat 1 g
- Saturated Fat 0 g
- Cholesterol 0 mg
- Sodium 201 mg
- Total Carbohydrate 48 g
- Dietary Fiber 19 g
- Total Sugars 1 g
- Protein 15 g
- Potassium 712 mg

Mango with Quinoa & Black Beans

Preparation Time: 30 minutes
Cooking Time: 30 minutes
Servings: 2

Ingredients:

- ½ cup quinoa, toasted
- 1 cup water
- ¼ cup orange juice
- ¼ cup fresh cilantro, chopped
- 2 tablespoons rice vinegar
- 2 teaspoons sesame oil, toasted
- 1 teaspoon fresh ginger, minced
- Salt to taste
- Cayenne pepper to taste
- 1 mango, diced
- 1 red bell pepper, diced
- 1 cup canned black beans
- 2 scallions, sliced thinly

Method:

1. Put quinoa in a pot.
2. Pour in water.
3. Bring to a boil.
4. Reduce heat to simmer for 20 minutes.
5. While waiting, mix the rest of the ingredients.
6. Add the quinoa to the mango mixture and transfer to a food container.
7. Refrigerate for up to 2 days.
8. Serve chilled.

Nutritional Value:

- Calories 419
- Total Fat 9 g

- Saturated Fat 1 g
- Cholesterol 0 mg
- Sodium 256 mg
- Total Carbohydrate 72 g

- Dietary Fiber 20 g
- Total Sugars 25 g
- Protein 15 g
- Potassium 964 mg

Chapter 8: Sauces and Desserts

Tomato Salsa with Marjoram

Preparation Time: 10 minutes
Cooking Time: 0 minute
Servings: 12

Ingredients:

- 1 clove garlic, minced
- ½ teaspoon salt
- 3 tomatoes, chopped
- 2 tablespoons white onion, chopped
- 2 teaspoons fresh marjoram, chopped
- Pepper to taste

Method:

1. Mash garlic using a fork.
2. Season with salt.
3. Mix the rest of the ingredients with the garlic paste.
4. Use as dip for vegan chips and crackers.

Nutritional Value:

- Calories 5
- Total Fat 0 g
- Saturated Fat 0 g
- Cholesterol 0 mg
- Sodium 81 mg
- Total Carbohydrate 1 g
- Dietary Fiber 0 g
- Total Sugars 1 g
- Protein 0 g
- Potassium 58 mg

Lemon Garlic Tahini Sauce

Preparation Time: 10 minutes
Cooking Time: 0 minute
Servings: 8

Ingredients:

- 3 tablespoons tahini
- 3 tablespoons warm water
- 2 tablespoons lemon juice
- 1 tablespoon olive oil
- 1 clove garlic, grated
- Salt to taste

Method:

1. Combine all the ingredients in a glass jar with lid.
2. Shake to blend well.
3. Cover and refrigerate until ready to use.

Nutritional Value:

- Calories 50
- Total Fat 5 g
- Saturated Fat 1 g
- Cholesterol 0 mg
- Sodium 75 mg

- Total Carbohydrate 2 g
- Dietary Fiber 0 g
- Total Sugars 0 g
- Protein 1 g
- Potassium 35 mg

Mushroom Gravy

Preparation Time: 10 minutes
Cooking Time: 10 minutes
Servings: 8

Ingredients:

- 3 tablespoons olive oil
- 1 cup button mushrooms
- 1 cup cremini mushrooms
- 1 cup oyster mushrooms
- 1 cup shiitake mushrooms
- Salt and pepper to taste
- 1 shallot, chopped
- ¼ cup dry sherry
- 2 tablespoons all-purpose flour
- 2 cups mushroom broth
- 1 teaspoon fresh thyme, chopped

Method:

1. Pour oil into a pan over medium high heat.
2. Add mushrooms and season with salt and pepper.
3. Cook for 3 minutes without stirring.
4. Stir and then cook for 3 more minutes.
5. Add shallot and cook for 1 minute.
6. Lower heat and pour in sherry.
7. Cook while stirring for 1 minute.
8. Sprinkle flour and mix to coat evenly.
9. Pour in the broth and bring to a boil.
10. Simmer until the sauce has been reduced.
11. Add thyme.
12. Store in the refrigerator.
13. Serve with mashed potatoes or cauliflower steaks.

Nutritional Value:

- Calories 70
- Total Fat 5.4g
- Saturated Fat 0.8g
- Cholesterol 0mg
- Sodium 45mg

- Total Carbohydrate 5.2g
- Dietary Fiber 0.7g
- Total Sugars 1g
- Protein 1.2g
- Potassium 93mg

Pepper Vinaigrette

Preparation Time: 15 minutes
Cooking Time: 25 minutes
Servings: 6

Ingredients:

- 1 red bell pepper, sliced in half
- 1 jalapeño pepper, sliced in half
- 2 tablespoons lime juice
- 2 tablespoons balsamic vinegar
- 2 tablespoons olive oil
- Salt to taste

Method:

1. Preheat your oven to 425 degrees F.
2. Place peppers in a baking pan.
3. Roast for 25 minutes.
4. Add to a food processor and pulse until smooth.
5. Stir in the rest of the ingredients.
6. Use as dressing for salads.

Nutritional Value:

- Calories 54
- Total Fat 5 g
- Saturated Fat 1 g
- Cholesterol 0 mg
- Sodium 50 mg
- Total Carbohydrate 3 g
- Dietary Fiber 1 g
- Total Sugars 2 g
- Protein 0 g
- Potassium 56 mg

Greek Salad Dressing

Preparation Time: 5 minutes
Cooking Time: 0 minute
Servings: 7

Ingredients:

- 3 tablespoons olive oil
- 1 tablespoon lemon juice
- 1 tablespoon red wine vinegar
- 1 teaspoon dried oregano
- Salt and pepper to taste

Method:

1. Mix all the ingredients in a glass jar with lid.
2. Refrigerate for up to 1 week until ready to use.

Nutritional Value:

- Calories 55
- Total Fat 6 g
- Saturated Fat 1 g
- Cholesterol 0 mg
- Sodium 83 mg
- Total Carbohydrate 0 g
- Dietary Fiber 0 g
- Total Sugars 0 g
- Protein 0 g
- Potassium 6 mg

Citrus Vinaigrette

Preparation Time: 5 minutes
Cooking Time: 0 minute
Servings: 12

Ingredients:

- 1 orange
- 2 limes
- 2 tablespoons Dijon mustard
- 4 cloves garlic, peeled
- Salt to taste
- ¼ cup olive oil

Method:

1. Squeeze juice from the orange and limes.
2. Add the fruits and their juices to the blender.
3. Add the other ingredients.
4. Blend until smooth.
5. Serve with salad or steamed veggies.

Nutritional Value:

- Calories 45
- Total Fat 5 g
- Saturated Fat 1 g
- Cholesterol 0 mg
- Sodium 106 mg
- Total Carbohydrate 1 g
- Dietary Fiber 0 g
- Total Sugars 1 g
- Protein 0 g
- Potassium 21 mg

Creamy Cashew Sauce

Preparation Time: 5 minutes
Cooking Time: 0 minute
Servings: 8

Ingredients:

- ¾ cup raw cashews
- ½ cup water
- ¼ cup parsley leaves
- 1 tablespoon cider vinegar
- 1 tablespoon olive oil
- ½ teaspoon low sodium tamari
- Salt to taste

Method:

1. Put all the ingredients in a blender.
2. Puree until smooth.
3. Refrigerate for up to 4 days until ready to use.

Nutritional Value:

- Calories 76
- Total Fat 6 g
- Saturated Fat 1 g
- Cholesterol 0 mg
- Sodium 90 mg
- Total Carbohydrate 3 g
- Dietary Fiber 0 g
- Total Sugars 1 g
- Protein 2 g
- Potassium 83 mg

Choco Peanut Butter

Preparation Time: 5 minutes
Cooking Time: 10 minutes
Servings: 8

Ingredients:

- 1 ¼ cups unsalted peanuts
- ⅓ cup chopped dark chocolate chips, melted
- 2 tablespoons pure maple syrup
- 1 tablespoon peanut oil
- ½ teaspoon vanilla extract
- ¼ teaspoon salt

Method:

1. Preheat your oven to 350 degrees F.
2. Arrange peanuts in a single layer in a baking sheet.
3. Bake for 10 minutes.
4. Transfer to a food processor and add the rest of the ingredients.
5. Blend until smooth.
6. Store up to 1 month.

Nutritional Value:

- Calories 201
- Total Fat 15 g
- Saturated Fat 3 g
- Cholesterol 0 mg
- Sodium 76 mg
- Total Carbohydrate 12 g
- Dietary Fiber 2 g
- Total Sugars 7 g
- Protein 6 g
- Potassium 195 mg

Ginger Cranberry Sauce

Preparation Time: 5 minutes
Cooking Time: 10 minutes
Servings: 10

Ingredients:

- ½ cup maple syrup
- ½ cup water
- 2 tablespoons lime juice
- ⅓ cup sugar
- 1 teaspoon fresh ginger, chopped
- 3 cups cranberries

Method:

1. In a saucepan over medium high heat, add the maple syrup, water, lime juice and sugar.
2. Bring to a boil.
3. Stir to dissolve the sugar.
4. Reduce heat and simmer for 3 minutes.
5. Add ginger and cranberries.
6. Simmer for 5 minutes.
7. Store in a glass jar in the refrigerator for up to 3 days.
8. Bring to room temperature for half an hour before serving.

Nutritional Value:

- Calories 83
- Total Fat 0 g
- Saturated Fat 0 g
- Cholesterol 0 mg
- Sodium 2 mg
- Total Carbohydrate 22 g
- Dietary Fiber 2 g
- Total Sugars 17 g
- Protein 0 g
- Potassium 350 mg

Apple Butter

Preparation Time: 5 minutes
Cooking Time: 45 minutes
Servings: 24

Ingredients:

- 4 lb. apples, cubed
- ½ cup sugar
- 1 cup apple cider
- 1 teaspoon ground cinnamon
- ½ teaspoon salt
- ¼ teaspoon ground ginger
- ¼ teaspoon ground cloves
- ¼ teaspoon ground nutmeg
- 1 tablespoon lemon juice

Method:

1. Add apples, sugar and cider in a pan over medium high heat.
2. Bring to a boil.
3. Reduce heat and simmer for 20 minutes. Stir every 5 minutes.
4. Transfer the contents of the pan to a blender.
5. Blend until smooth.
6. Put it back to the pan.
7. Add the rest of the ingredients except lemon juice.
8. Simmer for 20 minutes.
9. Remove from heat and stir in the lemon juice.
10. Refrigerate for up to 2 weeks.

Nutritional Value:

- Calories 51
- Total Fat 0 g
- Saturated Fat 0 g
- Cholesterol 0 mg
- Sodium 49 mg
- Total Carbohydrate 13 g

- Dietary Fiber 1 g
- Total Sugars 11 g

- Protein 0 g
- Potassium 62 mg

Chapter 9: Snacks and Sweets

Avocado Toasts

Preparation Time: 5 minutes
Cooking Time: 0 minute
Servings: 5

Ingredients:

- 5 whole grain crackers
- ¼ avocado, mashed
- 1 tablespoon black olives, sliced
- ¼ cup tomatoes, chopped

Method:

1. Arrange whole grain crackers in a food container.
2. Spread each cracker with mashed avocado.
3. Top with black olives and tomatoes.
4. Refrigerate until ready to eat.
5. Toast in the oven before serving.

Nutritional Value:

- Calories 211
- Total Fat 13 g
- Saturated Fat 2 g
- Cholesterol 0 mg
- Sodium 293 mg
- Total Carbohydrate 23 g
- Dietary Fiber 6 g
- Total Sugars 5 g
- Protein 4 g
- Potassium 424 mg

Sweet & Spicy Snack Mix

Preparation Time: 5 minutes .
Cooking Time: 18 minutes
Servings: 20

Ingredients:

- 4 cups mixed vegetable sticks
- ½ cup whole almonds
- 2 cups corn square cereal
- 2 cups oat cereal, toasted
- 1 ¾ cups pretzel sticks
- 1 teaspoon packed brown sugar
- 1 teaspoon paprika
- ½ teaspoon chili powder
- ½ teaspoon ground cumin
- ¼ teaspoon cayenne pepper
- Salt to taste
- Cooking spray

Method:

1. Preheat your oven to 300 degrees F.
2. In a roasting pan, add the vegetable sticks, almonds, corn and oat cereals and pretzel sticks.
3. In a bowl, mix the rest of the ingredients.
4. Coat the cereal mixture with cooking spray.
5. Sprinkle spice mixture on top of the cereals.
6. Bake in the oven for 18 minutes.
7. Store in an airtight container for up to 7 days.

Nutritional Value:

- Calories 92
- Total Fat 3 g
- Saturated Fat 0 g
- Cholesterol 0 mg

- Sodium 228 mg
- Total Carbohydrate 13 g
- Dietary Fiber 1 g

- Total Sugars 1 g
- Protein 2 g
- Potassium 28 mg

Carrot & Peppers with Hummus

Preparation Time: 5 minutes
Cooking Time: 0 minute
Serving: 1

Ingredients:

- ½ green bell pepper, sliced
- 2 carrots, sliced into sticks
- 3 tablespoons hummus

Method:

1. Arrange carrot and pepper slices in a food container.
2. Place hummus in a smaller food container and add to the big food container beside the carrot and peppers.

Nutritional Value:

- Calories 140
- Total Fat 5 g
- Saturated Fat 1 g
- Cholesterol 0 mg
- Sodium 264 mg
- Total Carbohydrate 21 g
- Dietary Fiber 7 g
- Total Sugars 7 g
- Protein 5 g
- Potassium 601 mg

Roasted Squash Seeds

Preparation Time: 10 minutes
Cooking Time: 15 minutes
Servings: 2

Ingredients:

- ½ cup spaghetti squash seeds
- ½ teaspoon olive oil
- 1 teaspoon maple syrup
- ½ teaspoon ground cumin
- ½ teaspoon ground cinnamon
- ⅛ teaspoon salt

Method:

1. Preheat your oven to 300 degrees F.
2. Toss seeds in the mixture of the rest of the ingredients.
3. Spread on a baking sheet.
4. Bake for 15 minutes.
5. Store in airtight container.

Nutritional Value:

- Calories 203
- Total Fat 17 g
- Saturated Fat 3 g
- Cholesterol 0 mg
- Sodium 74 mg
- Total Carbohydrate 6 g
- Dietary Fiber 2 g
- Total Sugars 2 g
- Protein 10 g
- Potassium 271 mg

Chips with Kiwi Salsa

Preparation Time: 5 minutes
Cooking Time: 0 minute
Servings: 1

Ingredients:

- 2 tablespoons kiwi, chopped
- 2 tablespoons tomato salsa
- 8 corn tortilla chips

Method:

1. Combine the kiwi and salsa.
2. Serve with tortilla chips.

Nutritional Value:

- Calories 158
- Total Fat 6 g
- Saturated Fat 1 g
- Cholesterol 0 mg
- Sodium 334 mg
- Total Carbohydrate 25 g
- Dietary Fiber 2 g
- Total Sugars 3 g
- Protein 2 g
- Potassium 122 mg

Melon Dessert

Preparation Time: 5 minutes
Cooking Time: 0 minute
Servings: 6

Ingredients:

- 4 cups melon balls
- ½ cup sparkling water (berry flavor)
- 3 tablespoons white balsamic vinegar
- Lemon zest

Method:

1. Mix sparkling water and vinegar in a bowl.
2. Toss melon balls in the mixture.
3. Transfer to a glass jar with lid.
4. Cover and refrigerate until ready to serve.
5. Garnish with lemon zest before serving.

Nutritional Value:

- Calories 47
- Total Fat 0 g
- Saturated Fat 0 g
- Cholesterol 0 mg
- Sodium 16 mg
- Total Carbohydrate 11 g
- Dietary Fiber 1 g
- Total Sugars 10 g
- Protein 1 g
- Potassium 241 mg

Mango & Strawberry Ice Cream

Preparation Time: 10 minutes
Cooking Time: 0 minute
Servings: 4

Ingredients:

- 12 oz. mango cubes
- 8 oz. strawberry slices
- 1 tablespoon freshly squeeze lime juice

Method:

1. Put all the ingredients in a food processor.
2. Blend until smooth.
3. Store in the freezer for up to 3 months.
4. Let it soften a little for 30 minutes before serving.

Nutritional Value:

- Calories 70
- Total Fat 0 g
- Saturated Fat 0 g
- Cholesterol 0 mg
- Sodium 1 mg
- Total Carbohydrate 17 g
- Dietary Fiber 2 g
- Total Sugars 14 g
- Protein 1 g
- Potassium 234 mg

Watermelon Pizza

Preparation Time: 10 minutes
Cooking Time: 0 minute
Servings: 8

Ingredients:

- ¼ teaspoon vanilla extract
- 1 teaspoon maple syrup
- ½ cup coconut-milk yogurt
- 2 large round slices watermelon from the center
- ⅔ cup strawberries, sliced
- ½ cup blackberries, sliced in half
- 2 tablespoons unsweetened coconut flakes, toasted

Method:

1. Mix vanilla, maple and yogurt in a bowl.
2. Spread mixture on top of each watermelon slice.
3. Cut into 8 slices.
4. Top with blackberries and strawberries.
5. Sprinkle coconut flakes on top.

Nutritional Value:

- Calories 70
- Total Fat 2 g
- Saturated Fat 1 g
- Cholesterol 0 mg
- Sodium 5 mg
- Total Carbohydrate 15 g
- Dietary Fiber 1 g
- Total Sugars 11 g
- Protein 1 g
- Potassium 196 mg

Roasted Mango & Coconut

Preparation Time: 5 minutes
Cooking Time: 10 minutes
Servings: 4

Ingredients:

- 2 mangoes, cubed
- 2 tablespoons coconut flakes
- 2 teaspoons orange zest
- 2 teaspoons crystallized ginger, chopped

Method:

1. Preheat your oven to 350 degrees F.
2. Put the mango cubes in custard cups.
3. Top with coconut flakes, orange zest and ginger.
4. Bake in the oven for 10 minutes.

Nutritional Value:

- Calories 89
- Total Fat 2 g
- Saturated Fat 1 g
- Cholesterol 0 mg
- Sodium 14 mg
- Total Carbohydrate 20 g
- Dietary Fiber 2 g
- Total Sugars 17 g
- Protein 1 g
- Potassium 177 mg

Fruit Compote

Preparation Time: 15 minutes
Cooking Time: 8 hours
Servings: 10

Ingredients:

- 3 pears, cubed
- 15 oz. pineapple chunks
- ¾ cup dried apricots, sliced into quarters
- 3 tablespoons orange juice concentrate
- 1 tablespoon quick-cooking tapioca
- ½ teaspoon ground ginger
- 2 cups dark sweet cherries, pitted
- ¼ cup coconut flakes, toasted

Method:

1. In a slow cooker, add all the ingredients except the cherries and coconut flakes.
2. Cover the pot and cook on low setting for 8 hours.
3. Stir in the cherries.
4. Transfer to food containers.
5. Sprinkle with coconut flakes.
6. Refrigerate and serve when ready to eat.

Nutritional Value:

- Calories 124
- Total Fat 1 g
- Saturated Fat 1 g
- Cholesterol 0 mg
- Sodium 10 mg
- Total Carbohydrate 29 g
- Dietary Fiber 3 g
- Total Sugars 23 g
- Protein 1 g
- Potassium 275 mg

Conclusion

Becoming a vegan may not be an easy fear, particularly if you are a meat-lover.

But if you will consider all the benefits that it can bring to your health, and at the same time, how this lifestyle helps animals, it would be much easier to set your mind to make the transition.

Remember, you do not have to do it drastically.

You can start gradually, and then by the time you have made the switch; you will start to experience all the wonderful benefits that veganism can bring to your life.

Enjoy!

Made in the USA
Coppell, TX
29 January 2020